All Scripture references taken from the KJV of the Holy Bible, unless otherwise indicated.

CAGED LIFE: Get Out Alive!

by Dr. Marlene Miles

Freshwater Press 2024

freshwaterpress9@gmail.com

ISBN: 978-1-963164-70-1

Paperback Version

Table of Contents

CAGED LIFE

Get Out Alive!

Freshwater

Freshwater Press, USA

For Sale

And the merchants of the earth shall weep and
mourn over her; for no man buyeth their
merchandise any more:

The merchandise of gold, and silver, and precious
stones, and of pearls, and fine linen, and purple,
and silk, and scarlet, and all thyine wood, and all
manner vessels of ivory, and all manner vessels of
most precious wood, and of brass, and iron, and
marble,

And cinnamon, and odours, and ointments, and
frankincense, and wine, and oil, and fine flour,
and wheat, and beasts, and sheep, and horses,
and chariots, and slaves, and souls of men.

(Revelations 18:11-13)

Caged Life

We see in the above verses that the Babylonian merchants are selling things. Among their wares are cinnamon, and odors, and ointments, and frankincense, and wine, and oil, and fine flour and wheat, and beasts, and sheep, and horses, and chariots and slaves, and the *souls of men*.

How can the devil trade in or sell the souls of men unless he has souls to sell? And how does he get these souls? Well, the devil comes, not but to steal, kill and destroy, so he probably stole the souls, killed somebody or killed something or destroyed something to get these souls. (John 10:9)

Know that if the devil is anywhere around you, he's going to try to steal, kill and destroy. He's not there to bring you anything--, no pleasure, no fun, no wealth, no fame.

Although this is what he tells you. He would have folks believe that he's there for your fun, for your pleasure, for your fame, for your wealth. None of that is true; it's a trick.

The soul of man is captured by the devil by any number of ways. Usually, it is by making deals with the devil, which are not really deals at all. But that man may not realize that until later.

When the soul of a man is caged, it really means that that man's soul, that is, his mind, his will and his intellect is controlled by a demonic *spirit* or demonic powers. He may not know he is being controlled or on remote by any evil power, he may believe that all the fun he's having is his own idea. He may believe that all that sin is his entertainment and that since nothing has happened yet, nothing is going to happen; he is so wrong. Sin is pleasurable for a season and that is the hook. So, all that fun/sin is enticing, and the sinner is enjoying him or herself, until they are not.

Yet, God tells us in the Word, to possess our souls, to prosper our souls. Which means we are to have a well ordered and a matured soul. We're not supposed to be letting go of it, getting rid of it, trading with it, allowing it to be stolen, or overtaken by any *spirits* or powers.

Evil men, evil human agents are soul hunters. These evil human agents are driven by evil *spirits* or evil powers that are soul hunters. Sounds like a fantasy, doesn't it? But it's not. There are any number of reasons a devil agent may hunt for a soul. Let me say here that hunting for a soul is in line with the devil answering God thusly:

Satan, where have you been?

Satan said he had been walking to and fro seeking whom he may devour. He might as well have said that he was looking for souls to buy and sell. Wouldn't a soul be the thing of most value on that list of things for sale? How much devouring can even a devourer do? The devil likes money, so wouldn't being a soul merchant be lucrative for him? A soul is certainly is worth more than cinnamon, which I can buy for less than $10. Saints of God all that other stuff is the cover, the beard for what is really for sale, the precious, priceless, God-given souls of men.

Who may the devil devour? Those who do not have the devourer rebuked in their lives. Sinners. Those who are carrying iniquity from their own sins, and/or the sins of their parents and ancestors. Spiritual sluggards--, those who are not prayed up and have a dry prayer life. Occultists and those who dabble in witchcraft. The defiled; those who are outside the Gate and therefor outside of God. Folks who are in the wrong place at the wrong time, such as those hanging out with bad boys and bad women who may be under judgment from God. Don't be in that car, when judgment hits. Don't be that building when Samson knocks the pillars holding it up, down.

Be sober, be vigilant; because your adversary the devil, as a roaring lion, walketh about, seeking whom he may devour. (1 Peter 5:8)

So, an evil agent may want to capture a soul to sell it. Or, he may want to capture a soul to sell it out – not caring at all what happens to it. That evil agent may want to turn a soul over to hell just to hurt it or torment it--, such as the vengeful seeking revenge for hurts and perceived hurts. He may want to capture a soul as a candidate for ritual or for death to either promote him or herself in the spirit, keep him or herself from being sacrificed, or to steal from this person, as in an evil exchange.

Know that souls and soul-selling is a big ticket item, so stay prayed up. Never think that just because you're not bothering anyone that they will not bother you. It doesn't work like that in the kingdom of darkness. There could be absolutely no known reason why a witch may want to choose you or any other person for their own evil agendas. You may have looked at them funny in the grocery store. You may have taken the parking space they wanted in the parking lot. You may be prettier or more handsome than they are. You may drive a nicer car than they have. Your kids may be smarter and cuter than theirs. Most likely, it is because they just don't like the Spirit of God in you.

Be serious. If you are going to put on Jesus, put Him on all the way so you will have strength to stand when enemy assaults come. Surely you know you will be hated in this world don't you? Marvel not, they hated Jesus first. It's better to be hated with power, than to be hated as a spiritual weakling, so stay prayed up.

Already Caged

All of us need to know that the souls of every witch and wizard, warlock, any worker of the dark arts is already a caged soul. They themselves have caged souls. It's ironic because many of them go into the occult for power, yet they end up losing the power or the God-given authority that God gives all of us just for being here on Earth--, just from having been born here on Earth, in flesh. Because of our birthright and birth situation, we are set in dominion, under, His authority, and that's a lot of power, if we appropriate the power of Christ.

Workers in the dark arts have sold themselves to the devil and have exchanged awesome power for less-than-awesome power. What they've traded is something for now that will cost them all eternity. Most who make this trade are aware that is what they have done. But we can imagine that there will be some who will be shocked to find out that the devil lied to them and there is fine print.

But these dark workers end up under demonic control themselves as they try to employ dark forces to control, manipulate have dominion over, steal, kill or destroy others. Irony. And it's a bad thing.

Signs of a Caged Soul

So here are the signs that a soul is caged. These may not be all of the signs but it is a very good start so you can judge whether you or someone you know or love that you are going to pray for is suffering as a caged soul.

1. Whenever something good is about to happen, something goes wrong somewhere. There is disappointment, non- achievement, failure, backwardness, failure at the edge of breakthrough and success.

If you are always waiting for the other shoe to drop, stop it! The other shoe doesn't have to drop. Where is your faith? We are in the Kingdom of God. We don't have to put up with this in the Name of Jesus.

I see manifestations of this second one, all the time in my dental practice--, crazy, worn down teeth and chewed up jaws. These people are having some horrible dreams and grinding their teeth; the bible calls it gnashing. Specifically, when the dreaming gets so demonstrative that there is talking out loud in your sleep, suspect Caged Soul. If the soul is caged, then the life is caged.

2. When a person knows that they should be much further along in life, but they are not, suspect Caged Life. When they're relegated to being beneath and not above, to being the tail and not the head, their life is caged.
3. When a person absolutely refuses to be saved, surrendering their life to Christ, that is a sign of Caged Life.

When the soul is caged, the person really is not in control of their own will anymore. Not only that, the *python spirit* works to make a person not hear the Word, accept Christ, or become converted. In this alleged cage where this soul is locked up, how do we know that it is not guarded by the biggest, baddest serpent ever? How do we know there is not a whole den of them guarding this soul to keep it from stepping this way, or that way?

By all this guarding and punishment for stepping out of line, more than likely, the victim has been programmed by the devil without even knowing it, without even realizing it to not be around or be attracted to or go for the thing or the person that's gonna deliver them. This is like behavior modification. They may shun what they actually need to get free. After all, do you think the devil wants them delivered?

4. If a spouse suddenly says that the person they married is just not the same anymore, their spouse's soul could have been captured.
5. When you cannot feel the move of the Holy Spirit no matter what.

The presence of God is life. If you can't feel God then you have a dryness and an emptiness in your soul, your soul could be caged, and this is because you are locked away from the presence of God. The devil has sequestered your soul, hidden it, actually. This will make you feel lonely, possibly depressed, unenergetic. Your emotions are in your soul. If you can't feel your soul like you used to, or you can't feel for other people like you used to, like you know you should, your soul could be caged, and you may just be becoming an emotionless zombie. Your humanity is diminished. Compassion is a function of the soul; if your soul is not working like it used to, or as it should, you may have a caged or captured soul.

Signs of Caged Soul in Dreams

6. If you are seeing slow-moving animals in the dream like serpents, snakes, tortoises, and snails, you could have a caged soul.
7. You are wandering in a thick forest--, lost, you can't find your way out. You could have a caged soul.
8. You are in a store, shopping all the time in the dream but you never buy anything. You just wander around and around in the store. You can suspect a caged soul and also you can suspect *spirit spouse*.

(There are links to books on *spirit spouse* and spirit children in the back of this book.)

9. Also, in the dream you are wandering and wandering, and you can't find your way home, that is the sign of a caged soul.

10. In waking life, if you have double or split personality. Nobody knows what your reaction to anything will be on any given day.

You've heard people say, *I don't know about that one; they come, and they go.* They may not need a prescription from a shrink, they might just need prayer and deliverance.

11. If you feel like or have ever felt like the life and your life's blood has just been drained out of you.

That's one of the same symptoms as witchcraft attack, but who do you think is trying to capture souls? The witches, warlocks, the devil, and his other human agents in the Earth.

12. In a dream, if you're unable to open a door to a room that you're in, that door

could be spiritually locked by an evil entity. A locked door? That's a prison or a cage.

- I declare, Father, every power that is blocking my way, locking my doors, and my opportunities, blow that power away, in the Name of Jesus, with the Wind of God.

If you're in a forest and smell strange smells, you are most likely captive.

13. Animals are coming toward you, especially strange animals.

That may mean that you're in the wrong location and that God did not assign you to go there.

- You need to pray. Lord, take me out of any wrong location, in the Name of Jesus.
14. You see yourself in a prison or jail in the dream--, that's a no-brainer, you are captive, living a Caged Life.

Why, Oh Why?

For what reason would someone want to capture a soul? Why would a human agent want to capture a soul? Well, that's their assignment. Or, maybe they owe the devil--, they probably do, because nothing's free, remember they themselves have captured souls and they're just doing what they're supposed to, what they're told to do by the devil.

They say hurting people hurt people? Well, captured souls seek to capture souls. When a person sins that person sells their own soul to the devil. Next thing you know, if they are unrepentant, they go out and recruit someone else to sin with them. Sinners invite others to sin. Hurting people hurt people. Sold out souls sell out souls. Without Christ, it is automatic. Folks automatically reproduce after their own kind.

Witchcraft is sin; case in point, that soul is captured or sold to the kingdom of darkness. Witches are soul hunters and are famous for selling folks out to the devil for their own gain.

15. Soul tied souls are captured.

Yeah, if you're pining away and grieving over a lost love, a lost relationship, a lost anything, career, business opportunity, anything, and you can't get past it, your soul is captured.

If you're hopelessly sold out, your soul is captured. Your soul is fragmented and captured. But we're gonna pray about this with the prayers throughout and in the back of this book, we're gonna get deliverance today. Amen.

Senior Moments

16. If you can't focus or concentrate, your soul may be caged.

Senior moments are not normal. People accept them, but they are not a normal progression of aging and aging well in the Lord. Therefore, suspect a caged soul or witchcraft attack. Whether old or not, whether in the gold years or not, people who are in the middle of a sentence but constantly--, not just once or twice, but very often forget what they are actively saying at that moment many times in a day, this could be a symptom of a caged soul.

The Apostle John lived and preached until he was 100 years old. Your mind should be sharp until you don't need it anymore. The mind is part of the soul, if it is under lockdown, it will not function properly. That soul could be caged, so we need to pray against the caged life.

You will want to pray for that person. This is what Psalm 23 is about when we are asking the Lord to restore our souls that means we want him to not just break us out of the enemy's cage that we got in through familial sin, ancestral sin, or our own sin, rebellion, disobedience, in Jesus' Name, put us back together. Restore our soul, Lord. Remember us, remember us. Put us back together.

17. Another clue that you may be living a caged life is that you see yourself as having a twin in a dream.

   Cancel every evil dream.

18. If you have dreams of being summoned out of your body: Caged Soul.
19. Hearing strange voices.

First you need to prayer-treat your dreams and your waking life if you are hearing voices. Pray fervently; this could be a slippery slope. Get some sleep because you could just be sleep deprived. Sober up. You could have been into some stuff you weren't supposed to be into. But if this persists, see a doctor. Pray.

Trapped

This is my opinion, but people whose souls are caged or imprisoned feel, and often feel like they're trapped. And they really are trapped. But, instead of looking at themselves, instead of looking at something spiritual, they look at the physical body and they think, *Oh, I need to **change who I am,** so I don't feel trapped anymore.* These people could make minor changes, if a surgical procedure can be considered minor. Others make major changes such as gender reassignments.

Folks, this is a *spirit* that has overcome a person usually because their soul is all the way captive and they are being reprogrammed spiritually.

After a while, with no voice to counter it, no deliverance, they start to believe and buy into the programming.

The devil is constantly doing scientific and medical experiments on mankind if they are captive. They are captive, what can they do to stop him?

Folks, we must all get delivered, stay delivered, and possess our souls in sanctification and honor.

Really, this is a spiritual problem, a natural solution, no matter how complicated it is, how complex it is, no matter how painful it is, no matter how severe, devastating, or dramatic it is, it will never fix the spiritual problem.

A natural solution will never fix a spiritual problem.

This is caged soul. Caged Life is a spiritual problem.

A person who feels trapped may look outside of their physical body, all around themselves, and find somebody to blame. They may find somebody to blame for their feelings of being trapped because they really are trapped. But if it's their soul that's on lockdown, not their body, not their life. Their spouse is not the one that has them trapped. Their souls are caged. Their lives are caged. The devil cages souls, no one else. God would never, ever. It is the devil.

Feelings of feeling trapped also apply to singles who may have been ensnared by the devil at an early age.

Me?

Yeah. Uh-huh. You. Any of us.

So, a person that's entrapped by the devil at an early age may think that people that they're dating will try to trap them, as into marriage. Well, you can't really be trapped again, because if you are caged and trapped by the devil, then you are *already* trapped. This shows up in the natural in the people who are running, running, running from marriage but they date very often. They think themselves clever to do this and not do what God says, which is to get married, be fruitful and multiply.

They are not clever; they are caged. In being caged they will have character flaws and unattractive behaviors such as a loss of compassion, anger issues and other things that repel people from them instead of drawing people to them. All the while this caged person is pushing people away, people are also running away from them because they are no fun to be around. How much Fruit of the Spirit do you think a caged soul has or can produce?

Probably very little, to none.

You are a caged man, or a caged woman, if you think that you gotta go from date to date and person to person and just drop one, get another one, drop one, get another one, another boyfriend, another girlfriend, one after the next because you wanna be free. And all the while, you're just doing the thing that caused you to not be free in the first place, to try to get free. That is ritual sex.

Ritual sex is because of being in captivity. Caged. You are assigned to do it, do you not realize that?

Yeah, we're gonna pray.

Just as there appears to be an idol *god* for everything, people of God, there is a demon for everything. Every foul, lustful, perverted thought you have that is not of God comes from the devil. These "thoughts" start out as, impulses, ideas. That is what opens the door to the demon, devil, *spirits* that come in to stand guard over your trapped, caught, captured soul.

Let's say they captured your imagination first. Now you begin to think on things that God said don't do and don't think about, but you do it anyway. By this time, you are captured and sitting in some evil spiritual cell somewhere. Your mind has been programmed to think on evil and demonic *things*.

All the while the **answer** to how not to get captured, how not to stay captured and how not to be programmed or owned by the devil is in the Bible. THINK ON these things.

Finally, brethren, whatsoever things are true, whatsoever things are honest, whatsoever things are just, whatsoever things are pure, whatsoever things are lovely, whatsoever things are of good report; if there be any virtue, and if there be any praise, think on these things. (Philippians 4:8)

It's kind of like the books, ***Eat this & Not That, Drink This & Not That***, only way more serious and way more important.

We are also told to cast down imaginations because if you think on a thing long enough you will do that thing or become that thing. All the while you may or may not realize that the original thought or imagination was not even from you and may not even be within you at that moment. But somehow the devil made it appealing, appetizing and made you desire to continue thinking on it.

The hook is baited.

For Sale by Owner

The Book of James tells us how sin is formed:

Let no man say when he is tempted, I am tempted
of God: for God cannot be tempted with evil,
neither tempteth he any man:

But every man is tempted, when he is drawn away
of his own lust, and enticed.

Then when lust hath conceived, it bringeth forth
sin: and sin, when it is finished, bringeth forth
death. (James 1:13 15)

And, this is different from shopping, how?
This is different from how the devil presented
the Tree of the Knowledge of Good and Evil to
Eve, *how*?

We see person after person fall because of sin. IN the media they call it immorality because they are not saved but even the world expects some level of morals and ethics.

People of God, we know this is sin. And, we know it because the purpose of the idea, the influence, the cajoling was to move a person to do something against God. The end game is always something against God whether it includes other people, another person, or not. A person could sin against God all alone, or with another, or with others. It depends on what you are susceptible to. It depends on what your bloodline was and is susceptible to. It depends on what appeals to you (*monitoring spirits* know you). Note that the verse in James says a man is drawn away by his own lusts. Whatever you lust for, *monitoring spirits* study you and that is how the devil sends in the exact, custom-made temptation.

Your lusts can also depend on what took your ancestors out--, most likely the devil will use the same thing since it is in your blood to behave just like them, unless you fully put on Christ. If you fully had Christ on, you would have already squashed this sin at the imagination or the idea stage. But like the guy who keeps sending me emails to try to tell me something, he says—you didn't delete my email or block me. For this reason, that guy still thinks he has a chance to make a sale. I'm not calling this guy a devil, but this is how the devil works.

While this idea is cast into your head, you're not alone. You are never alone. You may think no one knows you are thinking about it, planning in your head how to do it, imagining what it will be like, and planning how to get away with it, but you are being watched all the way, particularly because you are NEVER ALONE. Especially, if you are captured – and trust this, you are if you are planning sin. Sin is by invitation and sin is by escort, always. It is what some evil demon imagines and wants to do, but it has no body, so it begins to work on you.

All the heinous, grievous Law & Order SVU-type crimes are all by invitation and escort. You know I use the word, *sinvitation*. *Sinvitations* are being sent out 24/7, even to you. The devil even came to tempt Jesus, what makes you think the devil won't tempt you?

Jesus had a strong and proper response for the devil, so the devil left him for a season.

Folks who have no proper and strong response to temptations and sin have no walls and no doors up to resist the devil, so why should he leave. You are easy pickings. You are ripe, ready to be programmed and used for evil. You haven't deleted the email or blocked the sender, so he will keep sending solicitations to you. *Sinvitations*.

When you sin, you sell yourself to the devil, and often for free. When you have no defenses, no walls, no word, no prayer life, no praise and no worship to guard your soul from enemy assault, and you entertain devil ideas, you basically have a sign up that says, ***For Sale By Owner***—that is your soul is for sale.

I Can Do This

The day you said to God, *I can do this all by myself. I don't need Your guidance or protection I got this.* The day you thought you were big enough and grown enough to do exactly and only what you wanted to do that's the day you really said to God, *I got this.*

And, I'll tell you now that was the day the devil got this--, and you are the ***this.*** The devil's got you in a cage; he's captured your life. How long will he have it? Maybe your whole life, but maybe for a shorter time if you become aware of it and get deliverance. Amen.

I think of the married 40-year-old who sighed that he just wanted something *different.* He was a dissatisfied sort. He didn't clarify if he wanted a new car or a new house or a new suit for church. He just sent out bat signals in the spirit that says *anything goes*. As I always say, if anything goes, then anything *comes*.

Seems he meant sexually, he wanted something *different*. I guess he met a girlfriend or new wife or something. But the devil quickly took his order like he just drove up to the drive through window of Good Burger, where an evil representative says, *"May I take your order?"* In the devil's case, "May I pretend to take your order and then come back and force my order down your life without you even realizing that it is not what you ordered--, *you genius*."

This bored, married man was programmed and in a cage, in a caged life and being instructed by the devil to break up at least his own marriage, but maybe also another--, or two. The devil "fills his order" because he thinks he can conduct his own life on his own--, without God. After he sins, the devil will accuse him, judge him, convict and condemn him, and then the devil can go and accuse him before the Throne of God.

Captive-sighing man just got deeper into captivity and deeper into the devil's jail. Perhaps now he's in a prison within a prison.

Surely, you've noticed all these people, even alleged-pastors falling from Grace into *disGrace* are only the same report over and again of what demons are doing and have done in the life of a person – a man, a woman, it doesn't matter. It shows the mundaneness and the typification of man, especially after they all seem to fall for the same sin or the same sins. Those are the temptations of the Christ anointing that Jesus didn't fall for, so He walked in His anointing. But these folks fall for the same evil, the same devils over and again.

So, the news isn't reporting on people, in my opinion. The news is reporting on demons and what they are doing, but until we see through the people part of the report to see the spiritual part, how much can we learn?

Oh, the man who wanted *something different* was also a "pastor." It is so bad when one gets bored of God and godliness.

God says, **Behold I do a new thing**, so wouldn't the devil also try that especially to deceive a person? A person of God, especially a pastor, should know to devil proof prayers and not just throw anything out there like a child throwing a tantrum because he desperately wants ice cream, desperately. It is obvious that that the married man's evil sighing prayer from his flesh and the devil is lord of flesh. Here we go!

The Word of God says that we shall not want (Psalm 23), and that is a sure way not to throw the wanting prayers up and have them get caught in the second heaven, where they want to capture your soul. The second heaven cannot capture a prospered soul, it is too big for them; it is too powerful for them. But the immature, whiny, wanting, needy soul, that's game for them. Don't be game for spiritual predators of the spiritual or human variety.

In addition, a soul cannot prosper in captivity. Much like veal locked in a tiny pen, and it can't move. Tender and tasty--, and weak, too weak to fight demons off.

That new something that that man should have gotten was maybe to get his soul out of the cage, maybe get his soul out of jail. Get the soul out of the devil's cage.

Something different? I got this? Nope you got your soul caged which proves you can't *do this.*

Same Woman All Your Life

Before we continue, I want to give a shout out to the real men, the real men who know how to answer the question, Marriage--, how can you be with the same one person for the rest of your life? Those who ask that question look at marriage as the *cage*.

It is not.

I want to give you a shout out because you know what the answer is, man of God. And your answer is:

- I am delivered.
- My foundation is healed.
- I'm not living a caged life,
- I am not under any *spirits of lust*, and perversions.
- My soul is prospered; I do not want.
- I don't have a spirit spouse.

- I'm saved,
- I'm set free,
- I'm alive and serving God in Jesus' Name.
- I am here to be fruitful and to multiply as God commanded in Genesis.

Saints of God, that is called **normal**. That is how God created man to be. God created Adam and then gave Adam one woman. Did Adam ever say, God, where are the other chicks? Where are the other women? In today's vernacular, *Where are the other tricks, or traps?*

No matter, male or female--- *traps* they'd be. The perfect bait inside an open cage that will not remain open once the bait is taken.

We praise God for all the real men in the Kingdom of God. Amen. Hallelujah. There is deliverance for all the rest who can't serve God, mankind, and his own wife as God said he should. I won't call it *settling down*, like a dog circling and circling his bed before he figures out how to get into it. No, I will say these people, many of them men, are NOT STABLE.

Jacob declared that Reuben was unstable, and why was that? It was because of sexual sin. Reuben had slept with Jacob's concubines and that left him unstable.

Yes, saints of God I am saying that the sexual sin that you've committed that the enemy has lured you into has affected you, it has changed you. it has deposited demons, devils, idols, whatever you want to call them into your soul. The human soul is designed for the Holy Spirit, not all those other idols, therefore that soul becomes unstable.

Reuben collected demons from illicit sex and became unstable; case in point.

Those newly-arrived demons have *voice* and desire and want to drag you into more sin. Your soul is now unstable, so you are easier to capture, keep captive, cage and program for more sin.

We should be praying for more Grace, not more sin.

Sexual sin may feel good--, at least for a season, so you don't mind complying and sinning and sinning, and sinning. This is ritual sex and it feels good, until it doesn't. Hell will either come up to greet you and give you a taste here on this side, if you are lucky. But if you are not lucky you may not know for your entire life that all that fun has dragged you to hell permanently. For eternity.

Satanic prison is the worst prison ever because the owner of the prison is Satan. The warden is Satan. The prison is run by Satan and everybody, all of his minions and his agents. But we all have to realize that if anybody is in, if their soul is in the devil's cage, their soul is in hell.

The person's alive, but their soul is in hell. Their body is here on Earth, but their soul is in hell. Your body's here on Earth going through whatever motions it can go through in life--, something like one step forward, two steps back, like those frustration dreams you have when you can't really accomplish something that you're trying to accomplish in a dream. Or, it's that frustration of not being able to get out of a predicament or a situation in a dream. Yeah, except this is your real life, so it's way worse.

Even if your body is here and your soul is in hell, eventually what is happening to your soul will affect your body. This is called sickness, folks. Physical sickness has a spiritual cause. It says it in my Bible.

So, your soul is in this prison. It could be a prison of affliction or torment or pains and suffering, captivity, sorrow, bondage--, any number of things. And your destiny is on lockdown because you're being precluded from doing the things you're supposed to do, the reason God sent you here. Further, your star and your glory have been captured. We have to know what to do because this can be deadly.

Your business could be captured, it could be caged. It should be way more successful than it is right now. It's caged. Your marriage, if it even exists, is delayed. Maybe you don't even have marriage on your radar at all. Your soul could be caged. Your dreams, both your night dreams and your hopes for the future are detained: Caged Soul, Caged Life.

If caged, your soul and your life are being ruled and controlled by Satan, demons, witches, wizards, or evil marine powers.

Fragmentation

When your soul is fragmented that is some of Satan's handiwork and so he takes the fragment that he has captured to hell. Your mind and your intellect are in hell. What's your soul doing in hell? Oh, it's serving the devil well. *How so?* Well, whatever the devil thinks up, whatever he thinks for you to do,

Remember, he's programmed you, or gotten control of your program. He's got control of it. Just do what he says. And this may or may not be a glimpse of what hell will be like when a soul really goes to hell full time and permanently, most likely it's not. Most likely it's worse. As bad as this is, it's worse but when time is up, a person who has not received Christ is going to hell.

This is what happens there. Work, torments, work, more torments, and you work for the devil, doing whatever he tells you to do. Caged Soul, Caged Life.

You can go a little bit forward in this cage, but you can't go far. You can hop put you can't fly. You can walk, but you can't run, and your life is in *sloooow* motion. It's one step forward, two steps back.

Ideas and things in your head that you want to do in your life you can't seem to do them, and it's been years. Remember, your body is here, so you may not know you're caged, unless you are really in prison in the physical. That is the utmost sign that your soul is also caged.

Simply stating, **They can't lock up my soul**, is not true. That is what this book is all about. In order for a person's body to be locked up, first their soul had to have been locked up; things manifest from the spirit to the natural. We need to be binding and loosing, then we can get ourselves uncaged on Earth through prayer warfare, in the Spirit.

Let's say you are not in a physical jail or prison, but believe you are free and roaming about the planet. It depends on what kind of a prisoner you are. You may be spiritually tethered or chained and you can go so far – you know those two steps and then the prison guard yanks your chain, and you get back where you're "supposed" to be.

Or, you could be such a good prisoner you only have on an ankle bracelet, and you think you are freely moving about your life. You're not. You are still being monitored and as long as you keep sinning, the devil won't remind you that you are in prison and only supposed to be doing what he wants you to do, because you are automatically doing it anyway.

Church? You can go to one but make sure it's not a real church. It can be a fake or secretly occultic church. Or it can be an openly occultic church, but don't go to a real one where there is deliverance. Don't go to a powerful church where there is deliverance. You can go to an entertainment or marine church--, the devil has those and many times they look like real churches, they are not, but they are acceptable for you.

The prison guard will yank your chain for going to a real deliverance ministry. In that yanking you will be punished, something will hurt, and or something, or possibly someone will be lost to you. This is Caged Life.

There's a lot to fight and there's a lot to pray about.

What Comes Next?

Reality check: if you're in a cage or your soul is in a cage, what do you think is next? You better figure out how to get out of that cage **alive**. You're not a pet. The devil doesn't like you. I say it all the time. I'll keep saying it. The devil's not playing with you or planning to teach you tricks and give you snacks.

What do you think your soul and any of your blessings or virtues or gifts from God are in a cage *for*?

We said at the onset, the devil sells all kinds of stuff, like the souls of men. **You are for sale. You're for auction.** But what if you don't get sold? What if nobody wants to buy you, as bad as that even sounds?

Does steal, kill, and destroy ring a bell?

Saints, you need to get ready to bust out of that cage, break out of that cage, out of that prison, in the Name of Jesus.

First thing you do is you surrender your life to Jesus. You surrender to Christ. You run to Him if you haven't already. It is the only way out of the cage. It's the only way out of spiritual jail. It's the only way out of devil prison or caged life. And it's your only way into the Kingdom of Heaven because no man comes to the Father except by Jesus. Amen.

Jesus answered, I am the way and the truth and the life. No one comes to the Father except through me. (John 14:6)

Maybe I should clarify here that an unsaved person can get delivered, even from captivity, but to maintain that deliverance they need to be saved and conducting their spiritual life, in sanctification and holiness by help of the Holy Spirit, on their own. You can't live a sinful life and run to church to get it fixed and then keep going back to the same ~~vomit~~ sinful life.

Witches do that. They practice witchcraft and when they get in over their head, they call on Jesus or pray the Lord's prayer, hide behind some Scriptures and when the storm seems to have passed, they go back to witchcraft.

They are not fooling anyone but themselves.

So, after you run to Jesus, or as you're there with Him, repent. Fall on your knees and repent for all your known sins, genuinely. Ask God to show you where you're in sin because maybe you just don't know. Maybe your sin is hidden to you based on your culture or traditions, you may not know, without the Word of God, what sins you may be ignorantly committing.

Maybe you are not committing sins. Perhaps this door that the enemy has used to cage your life was opened by an evil or deceived ancestor years ago, decades ago, hundreds of years ago. But now you are feeling the hurt from it, you're feeling the ramifications of it. You gotta do the work. You gotta engage in spiritual warfare. You may have to fast and stay in prayer. You keep praying, you keep praying, you keep praying until this thing breaks off of you and you break out of that cage.

But God will buy me back from the power of
hell, because he will take me. Selah.
(Psalm 49:15).

And then we're warned in Proverbs
23:14 B that God will deliver you or the soul of
the person you are praying for from hell if they
do the work--, repent and get saved, do the will
of God, and walk in disciplines of the Faith.

Do This for Your Child

This is a warning for parents to teach your child, train your child, give them discipline so their soul will not end up in hell. Lead your child in the way they should go, put the Word of God in them so their souls will prosper so they are not needy, greedy, *wanting and begging little* children as they are when they are two years old. Wanting everything makes a soul easy to tempt, and easy to capture.

God sends warnings to us, and He sends us signs along the way before we unfortunately get captured, so we won't get captured.

Many of those warning signals are seen in the dream, far in advance of anything really happening. God has given me dreams as far out as a year before something was trying to happen against my life. Did I pay attention? Did you?

Do we know how long it was from Joseph's dreams to when his brothers were selling him as a slave to the Midianites? Logically, it seems the more important you are to God, the more critical the horrible, devil-planned event is against your life and your destiny, the more you need to get fasted and prayed up about it the further out your notice or notice may be. Not only that, Joseph had **two** dreams. Two or more means, PAY ATTENTION, this is very important. Some of us know that if we keep having the same nightmare over and over again it is to get our attention. PAY ATTENTION. Prayer-treat your dreams, the demonic ones, the evil ones, the nightmares to cancel them, and also the prophetic and good dreams to pray them *through*.

In A Cage

Seeing yourself in a cage in a dream, that's a really big clue. Feeling trapped. We talked about that. You can't move forward while in a cage. Your soul is caged, your destiny is caged. Your star may be caged, your marriage may be caged, your career, education, family, ministry--, any or all of it can be caged. If the part of your soul that you need to work any of those parts of your life is unavailable, that is caged, then your whole life is hindered, paused, delayed, or diminished.

Any **part** of the aforementioned could be caged. Sometimes taking one cog out of a wheel makes the whole thing not work. Taking a part or a fragment out of your destiny or life, may render the whole thing stuck on the side of the road somewhere.

Remember, a soul can be fragmented. It's usually the part that you sinned with. It's where the devil has access. The tricks and tactics of the devil vary. You could have fallen in love with someone, engaged in illicit sex with them, then you two split up and now you're soul tied with that person. A soul tie is a form of captivity. You can't move forward because you are still thinking about the past with that person that was your heart's desire or that set your soul on fire. Or, let's keep it real, you may never have been in love with them, maybe that person really *put it on you.*

Saints of God, I've warned you: If you are having illicit sex with a person, that person may not be all that's in the room or all that's involved in the sex act. Demonically-charged sex is still good to humans. It's bad for them spiritually, but it is good to their flesh. Too good.

Search your soul. Ask God. If you're in a dream and you're just waiting, waiting, waiting for somebody. That is a sign of stagnation, non-achievement and soul ties.

- I bind the spirit of excessive waiting and delay, in the Name of Jesus.
- Lord, break every evil soul tie over my life right now, in the Name of Jesus.

If you're having a hard life, suffering and you're noticing circular problems, cyclical problems, seasonal problems, and you're not coming out of certain problems, you are most likely living a caged life.

Another purpose of caging your life is to make you waste your time, to waste your life, and just to make your life in vain and useless. It is designed to make you miss purpose and destiny; to make you a failure.

- You need to pray, Father, any power that wants to put my virtues in captivity, in a prison or a cage or a jail, yielding me a life of difficulties, destroy by Force, by Fire, in the Name of Jesus.
- Father, I want to achieve destiny. Scatter the plans of the wicked against me, in Jesus' Name.

Also in the dream, seeing animals such as goats, hens, or bears in a cage should let you know that something about your virtues is captive somewhere.

In the waking life if you're struggling to prosper, and enjoy the blessings of God, somebody somewhere has locked up and blocked up your destiny.

If you're seeing the image or the face of a person in a bottle in a dream, or seeing yourself in a bottle in a dream, this means spiritual imprisonment. It could mean that their star is imprisoned, or their destiny has been programmed somewhere else.

- Lord Jesus, Father, any evil bottle assigned to lock up my destiny, let that evil bottle break now and release me, in the Name of Jesus.

Any person issuing a curse at you in the dream? It is obvious that you are being cursed. Folks, pay attention in your waking life as well. Don't let anyone just say anything over you that you agree with. Don't agree with curses. If someone speaks a curse over you but you don't reject it, cancel it, or negate it, it is as good as you agreed with it. Open your mouth and defend yourself! Defend your life!

- Father, turn every curse of my life, whether in the dream or in my waking life, into blessings, in the Name of Jesus.

Get Your Dreams Back

I pray, friends, in the Name of Jesus, that your dreams will return to you and you'll remember them, and that you get proper dream interpretation from a Christian minister who can interpret dreams properly.

Do not use random or secular online interpretation. Most of those interpretations are fluffy and will have you thinking life is great because none of those dream interpretations will indicate anything to you but flowers, success, happiness, and wealth. I know, I used to read those website and boy was I deceived!

You need to know what's happening for real, in the spirit to direct your prayer life and save your life from a caged life, in the Name of Jesus.

Satanic Prison System

Some common spiritual prisons are:

A prison of affliction, prison of barrenness, a prison of bondage, a prison of death. A prison of debt, prison of failure, prison of fear. A prison of generational curses, prison of poverty, or a prison of sickness.

There are custom made cages. And those cages are to attract you like cheese in a mousetrap. Whatever you like will be presented to you, in public or in private. If you are very sneaky, it will be presented in private, or the devil will allow you to think you, and you alone found it and you can chase it and catch it, have it, wipe your mouth and keep on going and no one will know.

Folks, *how* to get away with a sin is built into the temptation to commit the sin. The devil tells you in whatever way you can hear and understand that you will get away with this, no one will know.

Saints of God, if you are so adept at hearing Satan, why can't you hear and obey God?

So, the devil traps are baited and set to ensnare you, keep you locked in, locked down, and to do you the most harm. And to give you the most torment. They are custom made.

The *bait*? It could be a person for sacrifice, or it could be a seasoned demonic worker. Either way it's heinous and you don't want to get entangled with any of that. But you can't just *say* you won't; you will need a spiritual resistance to a spiritual trap; you can't just resist in your own flesh --, if people could, all those pastors wouldn't keep falling. If people could, all those people wouldn't keep falling into sin and falling out of Grace. If people could, neither you nor I would ever sin again.

Drop the Cage

Anybody could have a caged destiny, caged blessings, a cage education, caged marriage, or even a caged car.

And how can this even happen, you ask?

Well, you see, the enemy may try you out at first by just drawing a line, like a line in the sand and daring you to cross it. And if you're not paying attention spiritually, you might say, *Oh, well, I think I'm not going to go and do that anymore because something negative or something I didn't want to happen happened, so I'm not gonna do that anymore.*

That makes good sense in the natural, but in the spirit, you have to ask. What thing happened and who bought that thing that happened to you? You have to be very discerning. So, if you don't do anything to cross a line that the devil made, then he has succeeded in hindering you.

You have to discern who made the line. God will make a line for your protection. The devil will draw one to control you.

If the devil succeeds in the first line, then he will just draw you another line. Either because of fear and/or not knowing WHO drew the next line, you don't go past that one either.

What do I mean by this? I mean that something happens, and you don't pray about it and ask God about it or tell anybody, or talk to God about it. So you don't get counsel from wise people, such as other Christians. If you don't search it out to see what the Word says about this thing that happened, you don't fast, you don't do anything, you just don't cross that particular line anymore.

Let me give you an example. What if you give in the offering and then your car breaks? So you stopped giving in the offering and then your card didn't break anymore. That's the first line. I must say, now he's going to draw another line. Like a game of hangman; like a game of pain, man.

If the devil is successful, he draws another line. Let's say you pray for your husband every night, but every morning he's acting worse. That's another line. So you stopped praying for your husband. And when you stop praying for your husband, he started acting at least the same or maybe even better. That's the devil messing with him. Maybe he's got a caged soul, too. So now the devil draws another line and another line, all it takes is four lines, and now you're boxed in.

But you have to cross enemy lines, in the Name of Jesus. You have to walk over all of these lines. You gotta pray, praise, worship your way past the enemy lines. You gotta call on the name of the Lord. You gotta plead the Blood of Jesus because the enemies line shouldn't hold you back. Don't accept the enemy's limitations against your life.

Fight!

Now that you're boxed in--, you got 4 lines around you, --, a square. All the devil has to do now is drop the cage, and you're in prison. Now you and your *stuff* are on lockdown.

- Lord, forgive me for not discerning when to fight and when not give in regarding the steps I should be taking in life, in Jesus' Name.
- Lord, give me more Wisdom and discernment so I will know it is You who is restraining me for my safety and protection and not the devil hindering progress, in the Name of Jesus.
- In the Name of Jesus, I repent of all addictions, laziness, willfulness, disobedience that has caused any cage-like situation in my life, in the Name of Jesus.
- Lord, deliver me everywhere I need deliverance, in the Name of Jesus.

Caged Education

A person, for instance, has been in college for five years, 10 years, 20 years and they just go to school part time because they have a spouse and family now. Seems you just can't seem to get that degree or certificate. You can't seem to finish that program.

By Word of Prophecy: **I set you free to matriculate and graduate today, in the Name of Jesus.**

In the case of your education--, you have just broken the door off the cage.

- Cage: You must be blown open, now, by the power in the Holy Spirit of God, in the Name of Jesus.

People who marriage seems to escape, people who want to be married and they can't seem to be married: I bind every devil from hell that is holding you back from meeting the person that God intended for you and having a fruitful and fulfilling marriage, in the Name of Jesus.

(Recommended books on spirit spouse and things that could be blocking you from marriage are in the back of this book).

For those who don't think you ever want to get married, I unlock your mind. I unlock and I unblock your thinking, in the Name of Jesus.

I uncage your mind, in the Name of Jesus to the possibilities in the future that God has for you in Jesus' Name.

Caged Car

People who just can't seem to keep a car, they keep wrecking their cars or something else odd happens to their car. I had a friend whose car just suddenly caught on fire. For some, their car constantly breaks down, or their vehicles get repossessed. That's the devil trying to keep you in one place your entire life. You've got a caged car.

The devil wants to keep you in one place and not progressing. But you need your car for school. You need your car for your children. You need your car to get your kids where they need to go, to school, to the doctor. You need your car for work. You need your car for groceries. You need your car just to run your household, and for emergencies.

- I proclaim today, in the Name of Jesus that you will become a person who can have a car, own a car, drive a car safely and wisely to purposeful, non-sinful places, and you will **keep** a car.

In the Spirit, I see you receiving the full title, the full ownership of your car, in the Name of Jesus. This could be the case for some of you for the very first time.

Thank You, Lord, congratulations, you now own your own car. It's yours. Believe it and claim it. Pray that prophecy through for your life. Amen.

Thank You, Jesus.

Caged Homes

God gave us all a **place**, but the devil is going about caging houses, people's homes. You need first to repent of all addictions, laziness, willfulness, any sin that's caused any caged house situation, in the Name of Jesus.

- Lord, deliver me everywhere I need deliverance, in the Name of Jesus.

The Bible promises everyone a place to rest and a right to ownership. The Word says in 2 Kings and in Isaiah and Zechariah that we're gonna eat fruit from our own vine and from our own fig tree that grows on our own property. We shall also drink water from our own wells.

We can invite our neighbors over to sit under the tree with us. God has promised us that. God has promised us in his Word that we have a place. Even the birds have nests.

God made man from the dust of Earth, and he breathed life into him, and he gave him a name, he said him in dominion, and He gave man a place in the Garden. He gave him a place in paradise. Even though Adam lost it, we have been redeemed by Jesus Christ.

Everyone should have a house. Everyone has a right to have a place to call home, in the Name of Jesus.

- I proclaim by the power in the Blood of Jesus that you will have your own house, you will keep your own house, you will live in your own house, and you will own or sell your house and keep the profits and the equity when you're ready to move and not before, in the Name of Jesus.
- I bind the wandering, *vagabond spirit*, I proclaim peace, stability and steadfastness over you and your dwelling place, in the Name of Jesus.
- I pray to the Lord, El Shaddai to give you divine and regular provision of

more than enough to acquire, buy your house, pay for your house at regular intervals and maintain your house. Make it into a home for you and your family.

- And when it's all said and done, this house can be a good inheritance for your *children's* children, in the Name of Jesus.

- May the Lord give you knowledge and Wisdom to know how to handle all details associated with your home so there will be no surprises, no worries, no stress, in the Name of Jesus.

This prayer is anointed of God. I see some of you getting a second home, or even more, as investments, in the Name of Jesus.

Thank You, Lord.

A Cage Is Not a Home

I break every ancestral curse, every family curse that has run in families that has blocked anyone from getting a home, keeping a home, in the Name of Jesus,

I shatter the evil altars that are responsible for these curses, in the Name of Jesus.

Lord, send Your mighty angels with the Thunder Hammer of God to break up every evil altar, in Jesus' Name.

Lord, break every evil covenant and every evil curse, in the Name of Jesus.

I Bind every demon assigned to carry out the curses, in the Name of Jesus.

Lord, forgive any family member who brought this curse into the family line by the Blood of Jesus.

You promised in Your Word that we would have a place. Thank You, Lord.

I dwell in safety; thank You, Lord, for our homes, for our neighborhoods, for our communities.

I uncage every caged home right now, in the Name of Jesus.

Lord, a cage is not a home, we are not animals, in the Name of Jesus.

Lord, a cage is not a home, we are not captives, let us not be captives, in the Name of Jesus.

Lord, a cage is not a home, let us never be comfortable in a cage, but constantly work to get out and be restored to You, in the Name of Jesus.

Lord, a cage is not my home, it is a prison, let us praise like Paul and Silas, even at midnight that we may be freed with a mighty Earthquake, in the Name of Jesus.

Lord, no cage can hold me, let the Angel of the Lord, come and break these bars, and *loose* my bands and free me from this cage, in the Name of Jesus.

Lord, let the cage be unlocked, let the doors, even the bars of iron be opened that I am able to walk out of any cage, every cage, in the Name of Jesus.

I repent for my sins and the sins of my parents and my ancestors, in the Name of Jesus.

Lord, forgive my sin and my iniquity, in the Name of Jesus.

Lord, I call out any and every part of me, of my humanity that is hidden away, locked away, sequestered, even guarded like a prisoner, in the Name of Jesus.

Lord, spoil the spoiler; bind the strongman, Lord Jesus with all Force necessary, do not leave my soul in this cage, do not leave my soul in hell, in the Name of Jesus.

Loose me, *loose* me, *loose* me, in the Name of Jesus.

Untie me, in the Name of Jesus.

Lord, put me back together, in the Name of Jesus.

Lord, restore me. Help me be gathered together again, in the Name of Jesus.

Lord, give us the mind to work and pay fees or rent or mortgages for our real homes in the natural, in the Name of Jesus.

Mighty warrior angels of God, break every pot and every other container that cages every home for God's people, in the Name of Jesus.

Unearth every birthright blessing and remember every home and marriage that has been scattered by evil winds, in the Name of Jesus.

West wind of God, O restoring wind of God, blow back together, every home of God's people, in the Name of Jesus.

Lord, open every lock, every padlock that locks every home from God's people, in the Name of Jesus.

Lord, break down every wall and gate and door and barrier in every realm, age, timeline, dimension, and across every access point, in the Name of Jesus.

Break Me Out

Father, break me out of every evil timeline that I either mistakenly, willfully, or in ignorance walked into, in the Name of Jesus.

Lord, put me in the timeline of the righteous scroll that You prepared for me from before my conception, so I may reach my destined future, in the Name of Jesus.

Lord, perfect those matters that concern me, in Jesus' Name, Amen.

I repent of all addictions, laziness and sin that has caused any caged house situation to come upon me, in the Name of Jesus.

Lord, forgive me and heal me, in the Name of Jesus.

Lord, deliver me everywhere I need deliverance, in the Name of Jesus.

Father, break the curse of bad housing and bad housing situations off my family bloodline, in the name of Jesus.

Father, break the curse of bad landlords, slumlords, tenement housing, in the Name of Jesus.

A cage is not a home. A cage is not my home, in the Name of Jesus.

Father, break the curse of unfair banking practices so that the people of God can buy houses, in the Name of Jesus.

I break the curse of Red Lining, in the Name of Jesus.

Lord, I break the curse of caged people being swindled out of money and property, in the Name of Jesus.

Lord, I speak of good housing, and I boast in You of good housing, good neighborhoods, good neighbors, good plumbing, good utilities and other services and amenities, in the Name of Jesus.

May we always dwell in safety, away from gangs and other evil activities of the night, especially in the Spirit and in the natural, in the Name of Jesus.

Lord, the time has come for Your fury to be unleashed against the enemy that blocks and keeps and takes people's houses away from them, in the Name of Jesus.

Reverse every curse of the people of God; they have been suffering far too long, reverse every house curse, in the Name of Jesus.

Lord, break every caged house out of its cage, in the Name of Jesus.

Send Holy Ghost Earthquake, Father and blow open the prison doors and *loose* every house, every home, every apartment, any type of dwelling place that You have for Your people, in the Name of Jesus.

Condos, townhouses, whatever You have for them--, loose them, make them available for Your People, in the Name of Jesus.

Let them have a real place in the natural to call home, to lay their head, to worship and adore You, in the Name of Jesus.

Cyclical problems with home ownerships or home loss, threats of home loss, worry, anxiety, stress, especially for seniors, and the aged, widows and the oppressed single parents, Lord, bless them to stay in their homes, bless them to own their homes, bless them to live in and use and rent out their homes if that's what they want to do, or to sell their own homes as they see fit, and get a fair and honest price for it, in the Name of Jesus.

Father, now that this home is uncaged, I cover the key to this uncaged house with the Blood of Jesus. Lord, give it to Your beloved and let them hide it where no enemy of God can ever touch it, in the Name of Jesus.

Make this key, this lock, the very deed to this house, too hot for the enemy to even want to touch it, in the Name of Jesus.

Hide this key in the cleft of the Rock so it's no longer a target for the enemies of God.

Lord, give us Wisdom and ears to hear and a heart of obedience to do as You say to remain in our hones, in the Name of Jesus.

Lord, the time has come to favor Zion; favor Your people, in the Name of Jesus.

Turn all *di*sfavor to favor today, in the Name of Jesus. Amen.

The Shalom

Lord, I dwell in safety, no evil shall befall me or my dwelling, in the Name of Jesus.

I pray the peace of God over your homes. I plead the Blood of Jesus over your houses and may the Lord bring the Spirit of Peace into your home, in the Name of Jesus.

May the angels of God be always welcome there, and may the Holy Spirit also take up residence in your home with you as you worship and serve the Lord and pray with your family, in the Name of Jesus.

Lord, every power pursuing my destiny, die, in the Name of Jesus.

Every power that wants my life caged, die, in the Name of Jesus.

Every power that wants my soul caged, die, in the Name of Jesus.

Every power that wants any of my blessings caged, die, in the Name of Jesus.

Any power that wants my health caged, die, in the Name of Jesus.

Lord, break me out of every constriction, in the Name of Jesus.

Lord, as you broke Peter out of jail in the Book of Acts--, You sent an Angel to rescue him. Thank You for your mighty warrior angels to rescue us.

You broke Paul and Silas out of prison. Father, throw open the prison doors. Throw open the doors of every cage, in the Name of Jesus.

Lord, from every cage of affliction and death and loss, I take my freedom now, in the Name of Jesus.

Lord, uncage every blessing, in the Name of Jesus.

Lord, let the trap of Jesus ensnare and arrest every trap set against my soul, in the Name of Jesus.

Every soul hunter and soul arrester be arrested, in the Name of Jesus.

My placenta be released from every cage, in the Name of Jesus.

I possess all my blessings, in the Name of Jesus.

God, arise and contend with those who are contending with me, in the Name of Jesus.

God arise and fight for me. Lord, fight those who are fighting me, in the Name of Jesus.

All those who seek my life, I command you to receive double disgrace, double destruction, in the Name of Jesus.

Lord, bring to light every darkness blocking my potential, in the Name of Jesus.

I break every curse of backwardness, in the Name of Jesus.

Father, thank You for setting me free:

My destiny, my star. Purpose, my ministry, my marriage, my family, my education, my career, my house, all my belongings and future belongings, are now set free from every satanic prison, in Jesus' Name.

Lord, arrest all soul traders, in the Name of Jesus.

Father, search the land of the living and the dead and gather every fragment of my soul, in the Name of Jesus.

Lord, rescue my soul from hell, in the Name of Jesus.

Ministering Spirits of God, wash me with Living Water and wash my rescued soul parts by the washing of the water of the Word.

Wash my fragmented soul, feed me Bread of Heaven, the Bread of Life, and return my soul back to me, in Jesus' Name.

Lord, I promise to possess my soul in sanctification and honor. I promise to prosper in my soul, as Your Word says, so that I may be in health and prosper, in Jesus' Name.

Lord, restore my spirit, restore my soul, and my body, in the Name of Jesus.

Thank You Lord, thank You that I've not come into this world in vain, in the Name of Jesus.

All wickedness working against me, be scattered by Fire, in Jesus' Name.

Every wicked power blocking my progress, die, by Fire, in Jesus' Name.

Father, anyone that is locking up or blocking my destiny, let Your judgment be upon them, in the Name of Jesus.

Collective captivity caging my soul, my spirit, my body: Break, break, Break! and release me now, in Jesus' Name, Amen.

I pray every satanic agenda plotted against me is destroyed in Jesus' Name.

No More a Slave

Every evil timeline, every evil calendar, every evil clock, be crushed, in Jesus' Name.

Father, break me out now from every satanic detention, in Jesus' Name.

I am free from every satanic manipulation, in Jesus' Name.

Father God let every garment of the prisoner that the enemy has forced me to wear catch Fire, in the Name of Jesus.

I'm no more a slave, no more captive, no more a prisoner, in the Name of Jesus.

Father, thank You for angelic help that delivers me from the hand of every principality and power that is up against me, in Jesus' Name.

Father, uncage every cage caging my glory, my star, my destiny, in the Name of Jesus.

Lord let every cage and every would-be cager be scattered by Fire, in the Name of Jesus.

Father, every iron gate locking me out of my future and destiny, and blessings, lift up your head, by the power of the Holy Spirit, in Jesus' Name.

Every divine miracle, manifest, in the Name of Jesus.

Doors that lead to my breakthroughs open by Fire, in Jesus' Name.

Father, let every satanic guard or security assigned to monitor me, sleep and die, in the Name of Jesus.

Father, thank You for saving my life from the cage, from the spiritual prison, in Jesus' Name.

I shall live and not die. I shall declare the works of the Lord in the land of the living, in Jesus' Name. Amen.

Angels of the Most High God: raid every satanic warehouse housing my blessings and let those warehouses release my blessings to me, and then receive double Fire and double destruction, in the Name of Jesus.

Every prison of poverty, debt, lack, affliction, sorrow, grief, sickness, death, failure, shame, fear, spinsterhood, barrenness, bondage--, any prison that the enemy has put me in or prepared for me, receive Earthquake from heaven and scatter now. Be reduced to rubbish, in the Name of Jesus.

Father, sentence every enemy that is after my life, to life imprisonment **with** torment, in Jesus' Name.

Holy Ghost Thunder and Earthquake strike to death anybody, anyone making incantation against me at any altar or shrine, I suffer no witch to live, in Jesus' Name.

Arise by Fire and consume every household enemy, giving information about me to the enemy, in Jesus' Name.

Stop the mouth of every *evil spirit, familiar spirit, monitoring spirit*, and unfriendly friends reporting on me, in the Name of Jesus.

My Father, Lord, my creator, let every power of darkness troubling my life become impotent right now, in Jesus' Name.

Father, I delete my name from every prison file by the Blood of Jesus, in the Name of Jesus.

God, who delivered Paul and Silas from the prison of the enemy, arise and deliver me from every satanic prison, in Jesus' Name.

Every forest, rock, and marine demon assigned against me, fall down and die, in the Name of Jesus.

Every charm fashioned or burnt against me, be roasted by Fire, in the Name of Jesus.

I release *myself* from evil parental linkage, in the Name of Jesus, and by the Blood of Jesus.

Lord Jesus, manifest Yourself in my life by Your name, *Wonderful*.

Every bird of death assigned against me, fall down and die, in the Name of Jesus.

I withdraw the food and drink of my problems, in the Name of Jesus.

No evil family rivers shall flow into my life, in Jesus' Name.

I reject an unsettled, unstable life, in the Name of Jesus.

I bind the *spirit of the vagabond* and I *loose* the *spirit of stability* and steadfastness, in the Name of Jesus.

Every deeply entrenched problem in my life dry up to the roots, in the Name of Jesus.

I destroy the weapons of satanic night raiders and satanic liquidators, in the Name of Jesus.

Angels of God, with swords drawn, encamp about me and my dwelling place to destroy the night raiders, in the Name of Jesus.

Night raiders, I blot out my name from your list with the Blood of Jesus. Lose my address, lose my location, in the Name of Jesus.

Blood of Jesus, let every stronghold of failure be broken, in Jesus' Name.

Anything planted in my life by enemies, come out with all your roots, and die, in the Name of Jesus.

Undo the Evil

All mind programming while under soul captivity be undone, in the Name of Jesus. I have the mind of Christ and I desire to do His will, in Jesus' Name.

Lord, whatever that bait was that made me crawl into that cage, I curse it, I renounce the sin, and Lord make me resistant to that temptation ever again, in the Name of Jesus.

I break free, I break free from every captivity and cage established by the enemy of my soul, by Redemption's Power, in the Name of Jesus.

I declare and require that the enemy restore back to me 7 times all that he's stolen from me, in the Name of Jesus.

I bind all retaliation against this prayer, in the Name of Jesus.

Thank You Lord, that it is done.

We are free and we possess our possessions, the tangible and the intangibles, in the Name of Jesus.

Lord, You be glorified, be glorified. Hallelujah.

AMEN.

Dear Reader

Thank you for acquiring, reading, and sharing this book. May the Lord make you aware if you are under captivity of any kind or living a Caged Life.

May the power and the Fire of God break you out of every limitation, constriction, and cage, all to the Praise of His Glory.

In the Name of Jesus,

Amen.

Dr. Marlene Miles

Prayer books by this author

While most books by this author have prayer points either throughout the book or at the end, there are some books that are **only** prayers. You just open up the book and pray. They are listed below:

Prayers Against Barrenness: *For Success in Business and Life*

Fruit of the Womb: *Prayers Against Barrenness*

Beauty Curses, *Warfare Prayers Against*
https://a.co/d/5Xlc20M

Courts of Marriage: Prayers for Marriage in the Courts of Heaven *(prayerbook)*
https://a.co/d/cNAdgAq

Courtroom Warfare @ Midnight *(prayerbook)*
https://a.co/d/5fc7Qdp

Demonic Cobwebs *(prayerbook)* https://a.co/d/fp9Oa2H

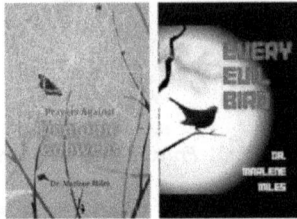

Every Evil Bird https://a.co/d/hF1kh1O

Every Evil Arrow https://a.co/d/afgRkiA

Gates of Thanksgiving

Spirits of Death & the Grave, Pass Over Me and My House https://a.co/d/dS4ewyr

Please note that my name is spelled incorrectly on amazon, but not on the book.

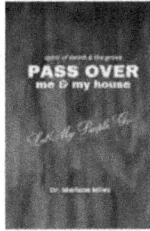

Throne of Grace: Courtroom Prayer

https://a.co/d/fNMxcM9

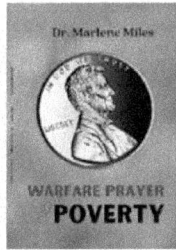

Warfare Prayer Against Poverty
https://a.co/d/bZ61lYu

Other books by this author

AK: *The Adventures of the Agape Kid*

AMONG SOME THIEVES

Ancestral Powers https://a.co/d/9prTyFf

Backstabbers https://a.co/d/gi8iBxf

Barrenness, *Prayers Against*
https://a.co/d/feUltIs

Battlefield of Marriage, *The*

Blindsided: *Has the Old Man Bewitched You?*
https://a.co/d/5O2fLLR

Break Free from Collective Captivity

Caged Life

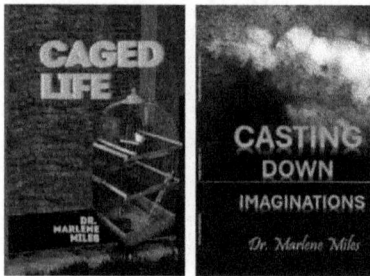

Casting Down Imaginations
https://a.co/d/1UxlLqa

Churchcraft: Witchcraft In the Church

Churchzilla, The Wanna-Be, Supposed-to-be
Bride of Christ

Curses of Blind Men

Demonic Cobwebs (prayerbook)

Demonic Time Bombs

Demons Hate Questions

Devil Loves Trauma, *The*

Devil Weapons: Unforgiveness, Bitterness,…

The Devourers: *Thieves of Darkness 2*

Do Not Swear by the Moon

Don't Refuse Me, Lord (4 book series)

https://a.co/d/idP34LG

Dream Defilement

The Emptiers: *Thieves of Darkness, 1*
https://a.co/d/5I4n5mc

Every Evil Arrow https://a.co/d/afgRkiA

Evil Touch https://a.co/d/gSGGpS1

Failed Assignment https://a.co/d/3CXtjZY

Fantasy Spirit Spouse https://a.co/d/hW7oYbX

FAT Demons (The): *Breaking Demonic Curses*

The Fold (5-book series)

- The Fold (Book 1)
- Name Your Seed (Book 2)
- The Poor Attitudes of Money (3)
- Do Not Orphan Your Seed (4)

Money on the Altar https://a.co/d/4EqJ2Nr

Mulberry Tree https://a.co/d/9nR9rRb

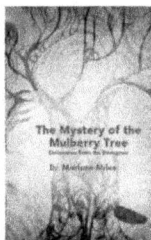

Motherboard (The) - *Soul Prosperity Series*

Name Your Seed

Occupy: *Until I Return*

Plantation Souls

Players Gonna Play

Power Money: Nine Times the Tithe

https://a.co/d/gRt41gy

The Power of Wealth *(forthcoming)*

Powers Above

Repent of Visiting Evil Altars
https://a.co/d/3n3Zjwx

The Robe, *Part 1, The Lessons of Joseph*

The Robe, *The Lessons of Joseph* Part II,

Seasons of Grief

Seasons of Waiting

Seasons of War

Second Marriage, Third--, *Any Marriage*
https://a.co/d/6m6GN4N

Sift You Like Wheat

Six Men Short: What Has Happened to all the Men?

Soul Prosperity, Soul Prosperity Series Book 3
https://a.co/d/5p8YvCN

Souls Captivity, Soul Prosperity Series Book 2

The Spirit of Poverty

StarStruck

SUNBLOCK

The Swallowers: *Thieves of Darkness*, Book 3

Take It Back

This Is NOT That: How to Keep Demons from Coming at You

Time Is of the Essence

Too Many Wives: *Why You Have Lady Problems*

Tormenting Spirits   https://a.co/d/dAogEJf

Toxic Souls

Triangular Power *(series)*

- Powers Above
- SUNBLOCK
- Do Not Swear by the Moon
- STARSTRUCK

Uncontested Doom

Unguarded Hours, *The*

Unseen Life, *The* https://a.co/d/0drZ5Ll

Upgrade: How to Get Out of Survival Mode

- Toxic Souls (Book 2 of series)
- Legacy (Book 3 of series)

The Wasters: *Thieves of Darkness,* Bk 2
https://a.co/d/bUvI9Jo

What Have You to Declare? What Do You Have With You from Where You've Been?

When I Was A Child, *I Prayed As a Child*

When the Devourer is Rebuked

https://a.co/d/1HVv8oq

The Wilderness Romance *(series)* This series is about conducting a Godly relationship and marriage with someone who is a Wilderness person. It is about how to recognize it and navigate through it. These books are about how not to get caught up in such.

- *The Social Wilderness*
- *The Sexual Wilderness*
- *The Spiritual Wilderness*

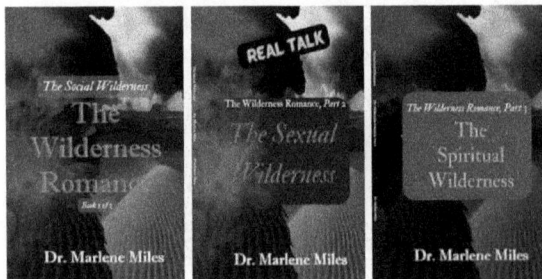

Other Series

The Fold (a series on Godly finances)
https://a.co/d/4hz3unj

Soul Prosperity Series https://a.co/d/bz2M42q

Spirit Spouse books

https://a.co/d/9VehDSo

https://a.co/d/97sKOwm

Thieves of Darkness series

Triangular Powers https://a.co/d/aUCjAWC

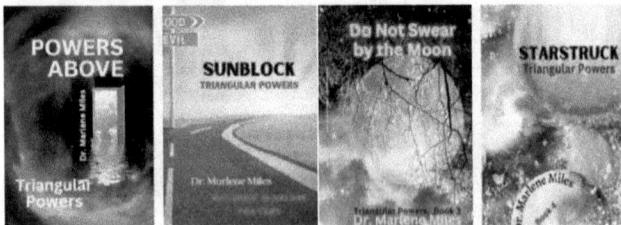

Upgrade (series) *How to Get Out of Survival Mode*
https://a.co/d/aTERhXO

  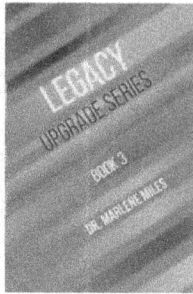

www.ingramcontent.com/pod-product-compliance
Lightning Source LLC
Chambersburg PA
CBHW062005040426
42447CB00010B/1922